To Share or Not to Share (Others' Data) – That Is the Question...

To Share or Not to Share (Others' Data) – That Is the Question...

Inaugural lecture
delivered on the occasion of accepting the position of
professor of Law and Economics
at the Erasmus University Rotterdam on Friday, 9 June 2023

Franziska Weber

eleven

Published, sold and distributed by Eleven
P.O. Box 85576
2508 CG The Hague
The Netherlands
Tel.: +31 70 33 070 33
Fax: +31 70 33 070 30
e-mail: sales@elevenpub.nl
www.elevenpub.com

Sold and distributed in USA and Canada
Independent Publishers Group
814 N. Franklin Street
Chicago, IL 60610, USA
Order Placement: +1 800 888 4741
Fax: +1 312 337 5985
orders@ipgbook.com
www.ipgbook.com

Eleven is an imprint of Boom uitgevers Den Haag.

ISBN 978-90-4730-169-1
ISBN 978-94-0011-328-2 (E-book)

Table of Contents

Dear rector magnificus,
dear deans and executive board
dear colleagues, students, family and friends
dear distinguished guests[1]

1 A Concern for Others' Data

To share or not to share – that is the question with a view to our 'personal data'[2] in the digital world. We leave traces of our visit when we access websites or conclude contracts online and buy (smart) products that collect and process our data while we use them. But also many of our movements in the offline world involve data sharing. When, if and how we share, and whether we are/should be asked about this at all, and when asked about it whether it is a true choice that we have, a true question that is being posed to us taken together, are a research conundrum of major societal relevance and strong interdisciplinary nature. Today I will take an (empirical) law and economics angle, with some reference to psychological insights. I will delve into data law and end on a more philosophical note.

Privacy is necessarily an interdependent matter.[3] I will focus today's presentation on a neglected topic, namely on 'others' data' that an individual shares, apart from his or her own data: so, actually: 'to share or not to share others' data – that is today's question'.

Examples of sharing others' data include genetic testing, which reveals data about whole families, voice assistants that listen in to conversations when you have guests over, programs that analyse all incoming

1 This booklet is an extended version of my inaugural lecture of 9 June 2023 at Erasmus University Rotterdam: 'To share or not to share – that is the question'. Therefore, some characteristics of a speech are kept.

2 For the purpose of this contribution I will follow the definition as provided in Art. 4(1) of the GDPR: '"personal data" means any information relating to an identified or identifiable natural person ("data subject"); an identifiable natural person is one who can be identified, directly or indirectly, in particular by reference to an identifier such as a name, an identification number, location data, an online identifier or to one or more factors specific to the physical, physiological, genetic, mental, economic, cultural or social identity of that natural person'. The terms personal data and data will be used interchangeably. Only when a reference is made to anonymous data is this specifically not personal data in the sense of the GDPR.

3 The first and still authoritative theory on privacy stems from A.F. Westin, *Privacy and Freedom*, 1967, New York: Atheneum; S. de Brouwer, "Privacy Self-Management and the Issue of Privacy Externalities: Of Thwarted Expectations, and Harmful Exploitation", *Internet Policy Review*, 2020, 9(4), 1, 4 explains the interdependency and mentions alternative formulations on p. 10: "networked, interpersonal, collective, social".

and outgoing mails or messages, group pictures shared online or much other household data: if I am getting married, my partner is presumably getting married, too. Another topical example is information that I may feed to ChatGPT:[4] for instance, my and the landlord's data in a letter I am prompting ChatGPT to write (think of address, bank account details or my and my partners' salary if I am applying for a flat). To differing degrees we can classify these examples of data sharing as 'direct'. In one way or another, individuals while sharing their own data give away data points about another or various other individuals, too. Apart from these direct variants of data sharing, data analysts also generate data about others in a more 'indirect' way through data mining and inference.[5] In this case, information about someone else is not directly shared. However, after having analysed data of a group of users, a program can learn about correlations. By looking at the friends in your social network who have revealed their sexual orientation, predictions can be made about you even though you did not reveal yours.[6] Male customers who enter a shop to buy diapers are apparently likely to buy a couple of beers, too, which is why stores put both next to each other.[7] While some inferences are funny, many are worrisome.

Today's presentation will consider both, situations of direct and indirect sharing of others' data – apart from my own.[8] It will not concern

---

4 See concerns about compliance with the GDPR as evidenced by the intervention of the Italian Data Protection Authority, *Registro dei provvedimenti* n. 112 of 30 March 2023; see the class action over alleged data theft recently initiated in the United States District Court for the Northern District of California by Clarkson Law Firm on 28 June 2023, Case 3:23 cv 03199.

5 J.A. Fairfield & C. Engel, "Privacy as Public Good", *Duke Law Journal*, 2015, 65(3), 385, 389.

6 Regarding Facebook, see M. MacCarthy, "New Directions in Privacy: Disclosure, Unfairness and Externalities", *Journal of Law and Policy for the Information Society*, 2011, 6(3), 425, 506 with reference to M. Moore, "Gay Men 'Can Be Identified by Their Facebook Friends'", *The Telegraph*, 21 September 2009, www.telegraph.co.uk/technology/facebook/6213590/Gay-men-can-be-identified-by-their-Facebook-friends.html (last accessed 5 July 2023).

7 See TDWI, https://tdwi.org/articles/2016/11/15/beer-and-diapers-impossible-correlation.aspx (last accessed 5 July 2023).

8 This differentiation shall suffice for the purpose of this contribution. There are classification attempts that go more in depth, see by de Brouwer, *Internet Policy Review*, 2020, namely into 1. direct disclosure about the other subject (e.g. blogging about people, but also giving access to Facebook friends' list), 2. 'indiscriminate sensing' (e.g. use of a voice assistant) where if one acts carefully the data sharing could have been avoided, 3. fundamentally interpersonal data (e.g. genetic data) where a link is inevitable and 4. predictive analytics (correlations generally found in data); see also O. Ben Shahar, "Data Pollution", *Journal of Legal Analysis*, 2019, 11, 104, 105: He distinguishes the intentional release of personal data (e.g. a data-driven ad on Facebook for elections/a political lie) and the nonintentional release (failure to secure the database).

cases in which one individual purely shares data about another individual.[9]

So, in the examples given, the question 'to share or not to share' is actually 'asked' to one person about another person's data? Apart from the decision about sharing one's own data, that individual effectively needs to ask him- or herself whether to share the other person's data, too. This – let us call it – 'responsibility' is clearer in the examples of direct than of indirect sharing. Individuals often ignore the effect of indirect data sharing.[10] Data sharing, or data disclosure, is done more or less inadvertently depending on the context, and hiding behind a lack of knowledge is quite possible. We may want to call the different occurrences a continuum.

In the continuation of my talk, I will first convince you of the social problem with sharing other people's data; in law and economics terms I will show you the existing market failure(s). I will talk about the different interests in this data and the trade-offs involved, just the same as valuation challenges and our experimental contribution (already completed or in the making). Lastly, I will criticise some incentives set in the current data law in light of our experimental findings. Throughout my talk I will keep the law and economics terminology approachable, thereby seeking to bridge some gaps between disciplines.

2 The Magnitude of the Social Problem and Its Different Angles

Our current data law is focused on individual autonomy (as it emanates from the fundamental right to informational self-determination) and puts the idea of consent at the centre, in accordance with the principle that individuals can determine when to share their personal data.[11] There are numerous legal and law and economics publications that rightly question the viability of this mechanism for the desired

9 In terms of the question who this data is shared with, this contribution is focused on the direct contract partner (a company) and does not delve specifically into the interesting question of how far these companies sell on data to third parties.

10 Fairfield & Engel, *Duke Law Journal*, 2015, 385, 391: "As long as the immediate benefit from disclosing your data exceeds the ensuing long-term risk for your own privacy, you will give away your data."

11 The conditions for lawful consent can be found in Arts. 6(1)(a) and 7 GDPR. We can label this the main approach. There are some other paths for lawful processing as enlisted in Arts. 6 and 9, and they shall be discussed in more detail in Section 5.

goal.[12] With a view to the sharing of others' data let it for the moment suffice to state that there is *de facto* a legal gap in our main data law, the General Data Protection Regulation (in short GDPR).[13]

This is problematic for a number of reasons:

From a legal point of view the first problem that comes to mind is a lack of autonomy and control over data-related decisions. I am not even being asked! Someone else *de facto* decides – more or less consciously – for me. We value a fundamental right to privacy that is being infringed with a view to the other person.[14] We can have doubts about individual empowerment. We can assess this behaviour against the principles of the GDPR: think of the principle of data minimisation.[15] The idea of collecting and processing data beyond the individual concerned seems to be at odds with this principle. Also, there is a severe conflict with the principles of fairness and transparency within data processing as far as these other individuals are concerned.[16]

As it happens more often than some scholars would admit, there is some harmony between the legal and economic insights with regard to an individual's behaviour. The law seeks to enable the individual to be in control and make an informed decision. Also, from an economic point of view we seek to enable individuals to behave such that they satisfy their preferences (to pursue utility maximising-behaviour) and here, if we are not even asked, there is obviously no opportunity to do so. Broadening the view from the individual to society at large in the law and economics world, a legal intervention requires an underlying

12 Fairfield & Engel, *Duke Law Journal*, 2015, 385, pp. 390ff; H. Skaug Sætra, "Privacy as an Aggregate Public Good", *Technology in Society*, 2020, 63, 101422: individualistic approach to privacy is insufficient (whereas being able to determine the level of privacy one desires stems from liberalism); M. Tisné, *The Data Delusion: Protecting Individual Data Isn't Enough when the Harm Is Collective*, 2020, Stanford: Stanford University Cyber Policy Center: EU approach ignores the collective dimension of privacy.

13 Likewise, Fairfield & Engel, *Duke Law Journal*, 2015, 385, 410 criticise that the individual is not always the relevant unit as the GDPR implies; de Brouwer, *Internet Policy Review*, 2020, 1, 6; A. Goldfarb & V.F. Que, "The Economics of Digital Privacy", *Annual Review of Economics*, 2023, 15, 267, 277.

14 See Art. 8(1) EU Charter of Fundamental Rights.

15 See Art. 5(1)(c) GDPR. We can speculate whether systems are designed such that the sharing of third parties' data is enabled/incentivised; see also de Brouwer, *Internet Policy Review*, 2020, 1, 10.

16 See Art. 5(1)(a) GDPR.

market failure. Otherwise, we do tend to place some trust in markets[17] – well, some of us more than others.

In the context at hand there are numerous reasons to intervene: the compelling market failure is a so-called negative externality.[18] A negative externality is problematic because an emerging social cost is not reflected in the product price. Think for explanatory purposes outside of the data context of a polluting factory[19] that does not account for the environmental harm it causes. The activity imposes costs on third parties that are unaccounted for. The price the company charges for its products would have to be higher if also all the environmental harm caused with its polluting activity were actually included – 'internalised' as we say. The same applies in our scenarios with people giving away information about someone else (who might not like that, in particular if this has negative financial consequences for him or her, or simply also dislikes the privacy intrusion). To stay within the transactional mindset, let us imagine that someone uses a voice assistant that listens in to his friends coming over in addition to his own words. Does this voice assistant ask you if this is OK? No. Have you ever been asked by a friend if it is OK that their voice assistant listens in before sitting down in their living room?[20] Most likely not … Are you

17 H.-B. Schäfer & C. Ott, *Lehrbuch der ökonomischen Analyse des Zivilrechts*, 2012, Berlin Heidelberg: Springer, pp. 78ff. In essence, a legal intervention in a market requires a market failure reasoning. This is particularly pronounced with the Chicago school. At the same time it has to be avoided that when intervening the governmental failure is larger than the market failure was. See D.A. Crane, "How the Chicago School Overshot the Mark: The Effect of Conservative Economic Analysis on U.S. Antitrust by Robert Pitofsky", *The University of Chicago Law Review*, 2009, 76(4), 1911, 1919; A. Ogus, "Regulatory Institutions and Structures", *Annals of Public and Cooperative Economics*, 2002, 73(4), 627-648.

18 Schäfer & Ott, *Lehrbuch der ökonomischen Analyse des Zivilrechts*, 2012, 81; A. Pacces & L. Visscher, "Methodology", in: B. van Klink & S. Taekema (Eds.), *Law and Method. Interdisciplinary Research into Law*, 2011, Tübingen: Mohr Siebeck, 85, 95.

19 Therefore, we see the use of the term data pollution, e.g. with Ben Shahar, *Journal of Legal Analysis*, 2019, 104; but also earlier D.D. Hirsch, "Protecting the Inner Environment: What Privacy Regulation Can Learn from Environmental Law", *Georgia Law Review*, 2006, 41, 1-63 argues how privacy law is similar to environmental law.

20 Some general terms and conditions seek to delegate this responsibility to the primary user, see de Brouwer, *Internet Policy Review*, 2020, 1, 8 with further references; the US-American notice and choice privacy system, so a system based on consent like the European one, is not able to handle these situations, see L. Bass, "The Concealed Cost of Convenience: Protecting Personal Data Privacy in the Age of Alexa", *Fordham Intellectual Property, Media and Entertainment Law Journal*, 2019, 30(1), 261, 290, 299 [however not referring directly to the third parties]; Amazon Echo recordings of a third party have been used in a murder trial (after the owner granted permission); see R. Davidian, "Alexa and Third Parties' Reasonable Expectation of Privacy", *American Criminal Law Review Online*, 2017, 54, 58-64, who argues in favour of two-party consent law, otherwise parties without knowledge of the voice assistant should have a reasonable expectation of privacy.

expected to anticipate that there is a voice assistant present when you visit your friends? Probably not (yet) … People contract over data all the time, albeit arguably with 'indifference to the data pollution problem'.[21] An information leakage[22] of this new oil named data[23] emerges – similar to an oil spill in environmental law terms.[24] The social cost imposed on others whose information is simultaneously shared is, for instance, not accounted for by the voice assistant and its primary user. The guests' harm is not internalised.

What does this harm consist of, more specifically?[25] Obvious harm that third parties can experience are the costs of the intrusion of their privacy, as such, but also true financial harm:[26] a commonly discussed phenomenon is price discrimination,[27] which means that a company charges individualised prices per user depending on their willingness to pay. Companies are really curious about this data for their pricing strategy and profit-making. It would then result that instead of a market price, consumers whose willingness to pay can be determined to be high will pay more.[28] Identity theft would be a very serious outcome of sharing others' data, too (if you shared someone else's ID

---

21 Ben Shahar, *Journal of Legal Analysis*, 2019, 104, 120 – emphasis in his contribution is laid on the effects of indirect sharing.

22 MacCarthy, *Journal of Law and Policy for the Information Society*, 2011, 425.

23 D.D. Hirsch, "The Glass House Effect: Big Data, the New Oil, and the Power Of Analogy", *Maine Law Review*, 2014, 66(2), 373-396.

24 Ben Shahar, *Journal of Legal Analysis*, 2019, 104 talks of 'data emissions' and 'data pollution'.

25 See, in general, MacCarthy, *Journal of Law and Policy for the Information Society*, 2011, 425, pp. 456-468: invidious discrimination, group injury, inefficient product variety, restricted access, price discrimination; M.R. Calo, "The Boundaries of Privacy Harm", *Indiana Law Journal*, 2011, 86(1), 1-31; Ben Shahar, *Journal of Legal Analysis*, 2019, 104, pp. 115ff; D.D. Hirsch, "From Individual Control to Social Protection: New Paradigms for Privacy Law In The Age of Predictive Analytics", *Maryland Law Review*, 2020, 79, 439-505, specifically for the case of predictive analytics (hence, the indirect sharing effect), classifies harm into the following categories: privacy invasion, manipulation, bias and procedural unfairness.

26 MacCarthy, *Journal of Law and Policy for the Information Society*, 2011, 425, 456-468; Calo, *Indiana Law Journal*, 2011, 1, 13 distinguishes the subjective and the objective dimension and T. Lin, "Valuing Intrinsic and Instrumental Preferences for Privacy", *Marketing Science*, 2022, 41(4), 663-681 distinguishes the intrinsic and instrumental preferences regarding privacy.

27 MacCarthy, *Journal of Law and Policy for the Information Society*, 2011, 425, pp. 462ff; Goldfarb & Que, *Annual Review of Economics*, 2023, 267, 273 (more weighted on the welfare effects); T. Friehe, L. Gerhards & F. Weber, "Keep Them Out of It! How Information Externalities Affect the Willingness to Sell Personal Data Online" (working paper).

28 H.R. Varian, "Price Discrimination and Social Welfare", *The American Economic Review*, 1985, 75(4), 870-875. In the most extreme case all consumer surplus is transferred to the producer. As part of the effect, buyers with a low willingness to pay will pay a lower price, too.

somewhere). The overall phenomenon is called 'data externalities'.[29] The concept includes direct data sharing of others and stretches to harmful knowledge that is generated by inference. To give a taste of their severity, *Ben-Shahar* goes so far as to claim that the external harms should be the primary justification for data law.[30]

What does the existence of data externalities mean for society at large? *Fairfield and Engel* 2015 argue that welfare economics shows that a suboptimal level of privacy is achieved in the light of data externalities. According to *Ben-Shahar* 2019, without internalisation excessive data sharing will likely result.[31] *Choi et al* 2019 show in a theoretical model an excessive loss of privacy when information about others may be inferred.[32] *Ichihaschi* 2021 models how if a firm can flexibly decide which information to collect, an inefficiently high level of data collection that harms consumers emerges.[33] *Acemoglu et al* 2022 argue likewise in the framework of externalities and, importantly, add an additional insight in their model on how externalities depress the price of data, which leads to excessive data sharing 'because once a user's information is leaked by others, she has less reason to protect her data and privacy'.[34] There is, thus, a consensus in the literature on the harmful effects for privacy. Note that the exact meaning that different scholars give to the term data externalities comes with some variation: for some it is the intrusion of someone else's privacy as such, while for others it is negative (financial) consequences that stem from it or any knowledge that is generated by inference. Furthermore, the harm can be linked to a third party, a third party group or public interests of society at large[35] (which, obviously, the third parties belong to, too): one example given shows that a cluster of physical

29 D. Acemoglu et al., "Too Much Data: Prices and Inefficiencies in Data Markets", *American Economic Journal: Microeconomics*, 2022, 14(4), 218-256; D. Bergemann et al., "The Economics of Social Data", *Rand Journal of Economics*, 2022, 53(2), 263-296; S. Ichihashi, "The Economics of Data Externalities", *Journal of Economic Theory*, 2021, 196, 105316; also termed '(negative) privacy externalities' by MacCarthy, *Journal of Law and Policy for the Information Society*, 2011, 425 and in some instances 'information externality'; termed 'privacy externality' by de Brouwer, *Internet Policy Review*, 2020, 1-29; Ben Shahar, *Journal of Legal Analysis*, 2019, 104: data pollution as a negative externality – he calls for 'data pollution law' (p. 149); de Brouwer, *Internet Policy Review*, 2020, 1, 3 lists additional related literature that calls the phenomenon differently.

30 Ben Shahar, *Journal of Legal Analysis*, 2019, 104, 112.

31 Ibid., 104, 107.

32 J.P. Choi et al., "Privacy and Personal Data Collection With Information Externalities", *Journal of Public Economics*, 173, 2019, 113-124.

33 Ichihashi, *Journal of Economic Theory*, 2021, 105316, pp. 15ff.

34 Acemoglu et al., *Economic Journal: Microeconomics*, 2022, 218.

35 Many examples of harm to public interests are, for instance, given by Ben Shahar, *Journal of Legal Analysis*, 2019, 104.

workouts collected in a fitness app can give away the location of secret geographic locations of US military operations threatening the public good of national security.[36]

In contrast to environmental pollution, it is noteworthy that, in general, sharing my personal data will also generate positive externalities for others.[37] For instance, new medicines could be developed that they can use as well. It can be simpler in the sense that you profit from a service improvement, such as music recommendation functions that some of you might enjoy[38] and that you have not financially contributed to. We can argue that these positive externalities increase if individuals share not only their own data but also that of others – for example, interlinked health or genetic data. Whereas it is acknowledged that both negative and positive externalities exist, the policy interventions required by the latter are less researched in law and economics.[39] A strict impediment on sharing others' data, too, would even make data sharing of things like genetic data impossible as this information necessarily conveys information about someone else. Generally speaking, as with the negative externality, so with the positive externality, there is a problem because the price paid is not accurate when it does not reflect the positive externality. We can record that both positive and negative externalities need to be accounted for in data markets. The more worrisome to scholarship are the effects of negative externalities, particularly if we wonder in whose hands the data can end up...

Externalities are not the only market failure that may be at play here. *Fairfield and Engel 2015* speak – interrelatedly – of both externalities and public goods, the latter being yet another of the classical market failures. If non-rivalrous and non-excludable, as privacy is, then the market will not produce (enough of) this good. Everyone can participate equally in it, whether they contribute to it or not. In other words

36 Ben Shahar, *Journal of Legal Analysis*, 2019, 104, 113 with further references.

37 Ibid., 104, 132, 140; Hirsch, *Maryland Law Review*, 2020, 439, pp. 454ff on the positive and negative effects of predictive analytics for others/the public; on positive and negative externalities, see A. Acquisti et al., "The Economics of Privacy", *Journal of Economic Literature*, 2016, 54(2), 442, pp. 445ff; Goldfarb & Que, *Annual Review of Economics*, 2023, 267, pp. 276ff.

38 Goldfarb & Que, *Annual Review of Economics*, 2023, 267, 277.

39 Notably, 'carrots', as opposed to 'sticks', compensate positive externalities; see B. Galle, "The Tragedy of the Carrots: Economics and Politics in the Choice of Price Instruments", *Stanford Law Review*, 2012, 64(4), 797, pp. 831ff: he gives an overview of how to remedy positive externalities.

free-riding behaviour is profitable.[40] The own contribution to the public good of privacy has a smaller benefit than cost and is, therefore, abstained from. My private benefit I receive by sharing (e.g. access to a website or use of a service) I consider higher than the costs (the ones I have due to giving up my data and the costs I impose on society by giving up others' data, too). Therefore, I share quite deliberately. There is a mismatch between individual and societal incentives. It is the existence of the negative externalities that harms the public good of privacy.

Another market failure we might see is an information asymmetry in the sense that the individual user that also shares other people's data might be unaware of doing so, not to mention unaware of the consequences this sharing could have for the other party. *Akerlof's* seminal article on information asymmetry concerns the inability of buyers of second-hand cars to understand the cars' quality.[41] Applied to the case at hand also, a 'polluting' privacy regime (in other words overcharging buyers by also collecting others' data in the process) can count as an unobservable product characteristic for the buyers. As it is not rational to read through privacy policies and the externality imposed on third parties is often hidden, someone with a privacy preference (say, for them and others) cannot see if a seller caters to it. This may impede a true market equilibrium. Companies may in the short run behave opportunistically and charge too high a price in the sense of reaping a lot of data points also about others.[42] Due to the information asymmetry, users will treat all sellers equally as they cannot determine if they actually have a more or less protecting regime for third-party data in place. Hence, 'privacy-protecting sellers' would not be rewarded.[43] It is not worthwhile for them to offer good third-party protection, and they will abandon these schemes. A market segment for privacy-conscious third-party data policies does not emerge. Linked to the information

40 Fairfield & Engel, *Duke Law Journal*, 2015, 385, pp. 414ff with further references as of pp. 418ff; Acquisti et al., *Journal of Economic Literature*, 2016, 442, 446 say the same about personal information; also Skaug Sætra, *Technology in Society*, 2020 argues how privacy is an aggregate public good and how it is the externalities that harm it.

41 G.A. Akerlof, "The Market for 'lemons': Quality Uncertainty and the Market Mechanism", *The Quarterly Journal of Economics*, 1970, 84(3), 488-500.

42 This is a similar reasoning to the application of an information asymmetry to standard contract terms, e.g. H.-B. Schäfer & P.C. Leyens, "Judicial Control of Standard Terms and European Private Law", *Economic Analysis of the DCFR: The Work of the Economic Impact Group within CoPECL*, 2010, 97-119.

43 The analogy is not perfect: We are talking about data rather than money as a price whose valuation is less clear. Furthermore, data subjects partially finance the service with others' data and not only with their own.

asymmetry, we now often see a reference to behavioural insights – so insights from the even more interdisciplinary field 'behavioural law and economics', where psychological insights advance economic thinking about the law.[44] Due to biases and heuristics, individuals are found to deviate systematically from rational behaviour that law and economics (and economics) traditionally departed from. Ask yourself, for instance, why you are more likely to buy fruit placed at eye level, a dress that is presented with a heavy discount or why you can easily be convinced to take out lots of insurance policies if that nice seller shows you all those pictures of natural catastrophes. So, on the one hand, it is argued that it is not rational to read through all the details of data privacy policies with a view to the potential costs – at least the ones we immediately perceive. On the other hand, there are explanations from within the field of behavioural law and economics for why users do not read the privacy policies: They might not be aware of the sharing consequences for someone else due to information overload (and sellers making only certain aspects of the transaction salient) or due to over-optimism,[45] thinking that nothing will go badly for them or someone else.[46] As part of the information overload scenario, there is also no understanding in how far others can be affected by my data sharing. This is, however, clearly the case. This omission is rightly accused of amplifying the negative nature of privacy externalities.[47] Some scholars go as far as claiming that the 'behavioural market failure' should be added to the classical law and economics market failures.[48] The emergence of psychological insights in law and economics has reduced the gap with purely legal scholars. If you wish, their emergence has made law and economics more 'humane' in the

44 F. Faust, "Comparative Law and Economic Analysis of the Law", in: M. Reimann & R. Zimmermann (Eds.), *Oxford Handbook on Comparative Law*, 2006, Oxford: Oxford University Press, 837-868.

45 On over-optimism: A. Tversky & D. Kahneman, "Judgment under Uncertainty: Heuristics And Biases", *Science*, 1974, 185, 1124-1131; Ben Shahar, *Journal of Legal Analysis*, 2019, 104, pp. 122ff also applies this concept to the topic of privacy: "People may indeed be over optimistic or overly pessimistic over harms that are equivalent to uncertain outcomes."

46 There is evidence that people show term-optimism with a view to Facebook terms when it comes to their own privacy; see I. Ayres & A. Schwartz, "No-Reading Problem in Consumer Contract Law", *Stanford Law Review*, 2014, 66, 545. It seems straightforward to speculate that they would be even more optimistic – if they think about it at all – about others not deriving harm from their actions.

47 De Brouwer, *Internet Policy Review*, 2020, 1, 4.

48 O. Bar-Gill, *Seduction by Contract: Law, Economics, and Psychology in Consumer Markets*, 2012, Oxford: Oxford University Press, p. 2.

sense that research is being brought closer to real human behaviour – slowly abandoning the idea of the *Homo Oeconomicus*.[49]

We have covered three out of four of the classical market failures. What is left is 'market power' – the classical justification for an intervention by way of competition law. Just briefly: Since we see sellers that gather large amounts of data (directly from users and their contacts and from data mining) on markets both with and without competition, market power does not seem to be the underlying market failure here.[50] Market power as an explanation would lend itself if we saw certain harm on markets because of the lack of competition. Therefore, the reason why we see 'polluting' privacy policies is not predominantly market power.

What becomes clear from the foregoing is that various market failures can be present at the same time. This needs to be translated into a legal intervention (a prohibition, a default rule, quality regulation, an information remedy…). It is challenging to decide which concrete intervention to advocate in light of an established market failure. The coexistence of various market failures – to varying degrees – complicates this exercise further.[51] In the continuation of this talk I will critically assess the chosen means of intervention – the GDPR – which in my view in its current application is defective for regulating data externalities – and seek to tailor it better to curing the established market failures, in particular, the occurrence of positive and negative externalities that have a direct link with the under-provision of the public good of privacy.[52]

49 Still, rational choice theory was not abandoned. Ideally, it is referred to the model – rational or behavioural – that best explains the behaviour, see R. Cooter & T. Ulen, *Law & Economics*, 2016, Boston: Addison-Wesley, 51. The models may give alternative explanations, see R. Chetty, "Behavioral Economics and Public Policy: A Pragmatic Perspective", *American Economic Review*, 2015, 105, 1-33.

50 See for an elaboration with a view to individual user data and the comparison of the market failure of market power and information asymmetry, R. van den Bergh & F. Weber, "The German Facebook Saga: Abuse of Dominance or Abuse of Competition Law?", *World Competition*, 2021, 44(1), 29-52.

51 W. Kerber & K.K. Zolna, "The German Facebook Case: The Law and Economics of the Relationship between Competition and Data Protection Law", *European Journal of Law and Economics*, 2022, 54(2), 1-34.

52 To a lesser extent, this contribution will look into how to cure information asymmetry and biases and heuristics with a better designed privacy policy.

3 Trade-Offs and Data Valuation Challenges

Economists assess trade-offs, and we do see quite a number of them here. There is an interest in the same data by various stakeholders; the membership of the stakeholder groups is, furthermore, overlapping. The most important players are commercial companies: in essence, by personalisation they can increase their profits.[53] Their products work based on data sharing by individuals, and it can sustain their competitive advantage in the market. Data is needed to be innovative and determines the company value. Companies care for clean and true data. While profit maximisation is still the norm, we increasingly see multi-purpose companies that also pursue social goals for which they likewise depend on personal data sharing.[54]

Then, there are the different data subjects. To start with, there are the sharing individuals. They are typically the users of a service for which personal data sharing is needed. They are the ones who access a website and, therefore, accept the cookie banner, the ones who 'get something in return'.[55] There is a lot of particularly experimental research seeking to identify individuals' valuations for data and privacy,[56] but the evidence is not conclusive yet. Experimental insights show how the perception of harm varies with a view to different types of data.[57]

---

53 Goldfarb & Que, *Annual Review of Economics*, 2023, 267, pp. 473.

54 Firms increasingly follow both profit maximisation and social goals; see R. Rajan et al., "What Purpose Do Corporations Purport? Evidence from Letters to Shareholders", No. w31054. *National Bureau of Economic Research*, 2023.

55 For the benefits of users, but also firms, see also Goldfarb & Que, *Annual Review of Economics*, 2023, 267-286; see Acquisti et al., *Journal of Economic Literature*, 2016, 442-492 for a comprehensive summary of the history of economic analysis on the trade-offs associated with privacy.

56 S. Athey et al., "The Digital Privacy Paradox: Small Money, Small Costs, Small Talk", No. w23488. *National Bureau of Economic Research*, 2017; V. Benndorf et al., "Privacy Concerns, Voluntary Disclosure of Information, and Unraveling: An Experiment", *European Economic Review*, 2015, 75, 43-59; V. Benndorf & H.-T. Normann, "The Willingness to Sell Personal Data", *Scandinavian Journal of Economics*, 2018, 120(4), 1260-1278; H. Li & A. Nill, "Online Behavioral Targeting: Are Knowledgeable Consumers Willing to Sell Their Privacy?", *Journal of Consumer Policy*, 2020, 43, 723-775 and various more. The seminal article on economics of privacy, see Acquisti et al., *Journal of Economic Literature*, 2016, 442, pp. 444.

57 See, e.g., Lin, *Marketing Science*, 2022, 663-681 on the valuation for different data points or K.A. Ackermann et al., "Willingness to Share Data: Contextual Determinants of Consumers' Decisions to Share Private Data with Companies", *Journal of Consumer Behaviour*, 2021, 1, 7, same as J. Cloos & S. Mohr, "Acceptance of Data Sharing in Smartphone Apps from Key Industries of the Digital Transformation: A Representative Population Survey for Germany", *Technological Forecasting & Social Change*, 2022, 176, 121459, 7 or J.R. Buckmann et al., "Relative Privacy Valuations Under Varying Disclosure Characteristics", *Information Systems Research*, 2019, 30(2), 375, pp. 377ff; J. Prince & S. Wallstein.

But also who receives the data, for instance, makes a difference.[58] In all these studies individuals' willingness to share their personal data is tested.[59] As stated previously, the legal rules work far from perfectly, but, at least on paper, the GDPR creates choice, information duties and purpose limitation with a view to this personal data.[60] What the GDPR omits is the data externality perspective. A common theme when we look into users' data and privacy preferences is the 'privacy paradox'.[61] It has been established that there is a difference between our stated preferences – so how much you say to value your data – and the revealed preferences – so how much you then actually invest in protecting your privacy (which we can determine in experiments but also looking at data from real market transactions), namely less than you stated.[62] Several solutions to this paradox have been presented, some of which question its paradoxical nature altogether. A simple explanation might be that the stated preferences were inflated.[63] After all, it is not so straightforward to come up with a monetary valuation of one's data.[64] This is challenging *ex ante* but also *ex post*, when data harm needs to be determined in a judgment, for instance.[65] In light

"How Much is Privacy Worth Around the World and Across Platforms?", 2020, pp. 5 (working paper).

58 Cloos & Mohr, *Technological Forecasting & Social Change*, 2022, 6; Ackermann et al., *Journal of Consumer Behaviour*, 2021, 1, 7.

59 To the best of my knowledge, the dimension of inference is not made explicit.

60 For details see Section 5.

61 S. Barth & M.D.T. de Jong, "The Privacy Paradox – Investigating Discrepancies Between Expressed Privacy Concerns and Actual Online Behavior – A Systematic Literature Review", *Telematics and Informatics*, 2017, 34(7), 1038-1058.

62 This is abundantly clear in an experiment by Benndorf & Normann, *Scandinavian Journal of Economics*, 2018, 1260, 1261 (with reference to previous contradictory statements), on p. 1264 they report the mismatch of stated and revealed preferences for their own experiment.

63 Benndorf & Normann, *Scandinavian Journal of Economics*, 2018, 1260, pp. 1261ff; Harrison and Rutström 2008 suggest a hypothetical bias that occurs when values are elicited in a hypothetical context, such as a survey; see also G.W. Harrison & E.E. Rutström, "Experimental Evidence on the Existence of Hypothetical Bias in Value Elicitation Methods", in: C.R. Plott & V.L. Smith (Eds.), *Handbook of Experimental Economics Results*, Volume 1, Part 5, 2008, Amsterdam: Elsevier, 752-767.

64 Accepting that it is difficult for individuals to determine their preferences and valuations for data, some scholars set anchors: in a recent experiment Acquisti et al., 2022 test different intervention to streamline the value of data when it comes to sharing the Facebook profile. In one treatment they informed participants of Facebook's projections of revenues per North American profile (namely, $400 per North American user in the next three years), and in the other treatment participants received information summarising the monetary compensation that some Facebook users received following the improper harvesting of user data (again $400 based on a real lawsuit Facebook settled), see A. Acquisti et al., "Information Frictions and Heterogeneity in Valuations of Personal Data", 2022 (working paper).

65 Ben Shahar, *Journal of Legal Analysis*, 2019, 104, 127 sees this problem for the data pollution context.

of the privacy paradox, should we compensate people on the basis of what they say or do?[66] Costs and benefits in the data sphere are hard to evaluate.[67] However, in the sense that *de facto* many online transactions nowadays exchange a product/service for data rather than money (or a combination), a transactional mindset does actually seem to be quite fitting.

To explain the paradox, scholars refer to behavioural insights to argue why users might still quickly accept the full cookie banner despite having a stated preference for privacy (e.g. if the less privacy preserving button is green and not red).[68] Avoiding data sharing is also made costly. Another explanation for the privacy paradox links directly to the externality dimension. *Fairfield and Engel* 2015 argue that even privacy-minded consumers will defect in light of the externality. Due to the overall behaviour of society, they expect their privacy to be lost, anyway.[69] Therefore, even though they state that they care, this behaviour cannot be observed. Along those lines *Ben-Shahar* 2019 argues that the data pollution explanation solves the privacy paradox in the sense that people do care about the social harm but not so much about the potential private harm.[70] The private benefits they find irresistible, and, therefore, they easily share.

There can ultimately be positive or negative effects for 'the other', let us say the 'data loser', that have largely been discussed when the externalities were illustrated.[71] We can hypothesise that the other, as every individual, may care about privacy and want a say in sharing. *Ex post*, they may want compensation for their shared, in essence leaked, data. Some may feel harmed by the intrusion into their privacy as such, while others may only perceive negative (financial) consequences as harmful. Note that the fact that someone else effectively shared my data may additionally destroy trust, for instance, in my friends, family and colleagues.

66 Similarly, Acquisti et al., *Journal of Economic Literature*, 2016, 442, 447: the price one would accept to give away data or the amount one would pay to protect it.

67 *Ben Shahar*, *Journal of Legal Analysis*, 2019, 104, 109.

68 This is considered under the term 'dark patterns'. For an overview of the different designs, see C. Krisam et al., "Dark Patterns in the Wild: Review of Cookie Disclaimer Designs on Top 500 German Websites", *Proceedings of the 2021 European Symposium on Usable Security*, 2021.

69 Fairfield & Engel, *Duke Law Journal*, 2015, 385, 425.

70 Ben Shahar, *Journal of Legal Analysis*, 2019, 104, 107, 112.

71 There may be harms to third parties and public interests that we are currently not aware of. This is an additional challenge in designing an incentive-compatible privacy regime.

Society, as such, also has an interest in data. It values innovation enabled by data processing, so do users after all.[72] It seeks to further data-based AI products used for the social good – which may not be the rule. Similarly, large data sets (including big data) allow us to develop better cures for diseases, for instance. But the discussed negative effects are also possible on various public goods that society values, among which is privacy. Obviously, both sharing individuals and data losers form society. In law and economics research we seek to make society better off (with all the measurement problems we can imagine for this exercise).[73] The societal interest is, broadly and ideally speaking, the sum of all of its citizens' interests, their preferences (e.g. a high valuation of privacy or a low one).[74] It is indeed in line with these preferences that laws should, hence, be designed.[75] Then legal rules are efficient.[76]

To ultimately determine what makes society better off, we still need to have better knowledge of how individuals behave on data markets and

72 In the competition law context, the concept of dynamic efficiency is argued to alleviate the differences between the consumer and producer surplus because consumers profit in the long run from the R&D investment of firms; see S.C. Salop, "What Is the Real and Proper Antitrust Welfare Standard? Answer: The True Consumer Welfare Standard", *Loyola Consumer Law Review*, 2010, 22, 336, 349.

73 The classical criteria in law and economics that are used to assess an improvement in welfare are the *Pareto* criterion and the *Kaldor-Hicks* criterion; see W. Pareto, *Manual of Political Economy*, 1906, Oxford: Oxford University Press; N. Kaldor, "Welfare Propositions of Economics and Interpersonal Comparisons of Utility", *The Economic Journal*, 1939, 49, 549-552; J.R. Hicks, "The Foundations of Welfare Economics", *The Economic Journal*, 1939, 49, 696-712. Both have pitfalls. In short, whereas Pareto is unrealistic since it requires unanimity in the sense that everyone wins. Kaldor-Hicks looks at a ratio between winners and losers – like a cost-benefit analysis – and, hence, is more practical. However, actually compensating losers (which must in theory be possible, otherwise there is no net gain) is not part of the theorem. Most economists agree, though, that redistribution is an important second step; see Cooter & Ulen, *Law & Economics*, 2016, 4: "While almost all economists favor changes that increase efficiency, some economists take sides in disputes about distribution and others do not take sides." Both criteria suffer from the weakness that the initial allocation is taken as given and may be very unfair.

74 There are many measurement problems in assessing individuals' utility and comparing it with that of others, aggregating it. A typical standard is the 'willingness to pay', see E.V. Towfigh, "The Economic Paradigm", in: E.V. Towfigh & N. Petersen (Eds.), *Economic Methods for Lawyers*, 2015, Cheltenham & Massachusetts: Edward Elgar Publishing, 18, 22. Other attempts to assess utility exist as well: e.g. happiness studies, auctions.

75 That is not such a straightforward task. See for the provision of consumer public goods, D. Lewinsohn-Zamir, "Consumer Preferences, Citizen Preferences, and the Provision of Public Goods", *Yale Law Journal*, 1998, 108(2), 377-406, who, among other things, discusses different preferences that may be displayed depending on whether you ask people in their capacity as consumers or citizens. Also in the scenario at hand, individuals can have various characteristics, e.g. be users and have a company, at the same time.

76 Let us clarify here that the term 'efficiency', in essence, means that we maximise social welfare. Social welfare is loosely spoken as the sum of all individual utilities.

of what they want: What are the individuals' data and privacy valuations and preferences? This is particularly true for the data externality dimension. Here, we lack insights into the valuations of others' data for both the sharing individual and the data loser. One established and important piece of evidence to learn more about preferences is experimental research, where in an incentivised setting – that means that you are paid depending on the choices made during the experiment and, therefore, show true behaviour – individual behaviour is tested and observed.[77] I devoted part of my research agenda in the last few years to furthering insights on individual data preferences by way of experimental research. My approach is, thus, more on the side of positive law and economics, seeking to identify individual behaviour rather than the normative side – however, the insights can inform the normative side.[78] Only if we know how individuals value their privacy can we formulate a fitting economic policy of privacy.[79]

4 Experimental Contribution to Learn More About Individual Preferences

My current research in interdisciplinary and international research teams tackles various open questions when it comes to data preferences. Various scholars argue that the sharing individuals do not care about the repercussions of their disclosure for others.[80] To start with, we put this strong claim that individuals are oblivious to data externalities to test in a sophisticated lab experiment:[81]

We designed an experiment in which individuals would with 0%, 50% and 100% probability share not only their own data but also that of others (the personal data consisted of the willingness to pay for an object, a lottery ticket to be precise). We explained in detail that sharing others' data would have detrimental consequences for the other, in the sense that owing to price discrimination a company could then

77 C. Engel, "Legal Experiments: Mission Impossible?", *Erasmus Law Lectures*, 28, 2012, in which he outlines the value of experiments for the law but also underlines that it is preferable that the outcomes of research pursued according to different methodologies point in the same direction before policy advice is formulated.

78 On the differentiation, see Pacces & Visscher, in: *Law and Method. Interdisciplinary Research into Law*, 2011, 85, 89f.

79 Benndorf & Normann, *Scandinavian Journal of Economics*, 2018, 1260, 1261.

80 Acemoglu et al., *Economic Journal: Microeconomics*, 2022, 218-256, Bergemann et al., *Rand Journal of Economics*, 2022, 263-296, Choi et al., *Journal of Public Economics*, 2019, 113-214, Ichihashi, *Journal of Economic Theory*, 2021, 105316.

81 Friehe, Gerhards & Weber (working paper). On the lack of empirical work on externalities that could guide policy, see Goldfarb & Que, *Annual Review of Economics*, 2023, 267, 277.

charge the other a higher price.[82] Using a so-called BDM mechanism (Becker-DeGroot-Marschak mechanism),[83] which allows us to determine individuals' willingness to sell, we could compare how much our subjects asked for their (and, if applicable, others') data.

We could show that people did care in the sense that they had a lower willingness to sell when others' data was affected, too. They valued data higher when it consisted of both their data and that of others. This counters the claims that individuals do not care, at least in a scenario like ours, in which the fact that others' data is being shared and what the (harmful) consequences of it are, are made clear to the sharing individual.

In our experiment we derived some additional insights by designing a treatment in which we first asked the participants to think about the social norm (by asking, 'What is the socially appropriate willingness to sell regarding the sale of information in your context?') before having them state their willingness to sell. This intervention notably reduced the willingness to sell, implying that the social norm is not to sell others' data or, at least, less than participants would spontaneously do.[84] As a policy relevant conclusion, there seems to be some potential in the reference to the social norm to reduce sharing and thereby decrease the emergence of data externalities.

Another result concerned peer information. In an additional treatment we intervened and told the subjects, after they had already stated their willingness to sell the data package, what the peer whose data they were possibly sharing and who was in the mirrored situation to share data including theirs had stated. We consequently gave them the possibility to adjust their amounts. In about 30% of the cases subjects adjusted their original willingness to sell. It is noteworthy that the effect is driven by an increase in the willingness to sell if the

82 The lottery ticket's expected value amounted to EUR 4. Indeed, empirically subjects' average willingness to pay amounts to EUR 3.91. Hence, compared with a random lottery ticket price with an average value of EUR 2, a substantial loss in consumer surplus was possible.

83 G.M. Becker et al., "Measuring Utility by a Single-Response Sequential Method", *Behavioral Science*, 1964, 9(3), 226-232. This works as a second price auction. The price the participants put is compared with a random offer. If the random offer is higher than or equal to the price, the participants receive the value of the random offer.

84 In our experiment it had quite clear negative consequences; the other party was charged a higher price – one can speculate that as soon as ambiguity enters the picture, and the negative consequences are less clear (or one can hide behind not knowing), the social norm might have less of a disciplining effect.

peer showed a higher willingness to sell. That means, in essence, that individuals follow the bad peer who does not respect others' privacy much. If someone showed a lower willingness to sell, thereby arguably signalling privacy consciousness, this signal was not honoured. Whereas it is a typical result in the social norms literature to follow the 'bad peer', still, it would be very worthwhile to further investigate how we can make individuals consider that someone is concerned about privacy. For the time being, presenting peer information seems to increase the (negative) data externalities.

There is, obviously, always a comparative dimension, in the sense that this is how our German subjects reacted; with Dutch subjects it might be a different story. Privacy preferences come with certain heterogeneity.[85]

Overall, and I am counting on this effect also today, presenting our experimental results in the past year had an element of an awareness-raising campaign about the situation of the other – which is not just the other but also you and me.

Another current research project of mine concerns the trade-offs between privacy versus functionality when it comes to smart products.[86] In essence, we want to measure how quickly people give up privacy if they get a good service for a smart email program in return. It is often claimed that users value functionality,[87] and it might be that they value it more than privacy. What is the exact cost-benefit ratio here? One interesting treatment in this experiment is to test how far it makes a difference if the non-privacy sensitive scheme is set as a default. Will then – as theory would predict and as it is experimentally shown in sticking with the default research in other contexts[88] – more individuals give up their privacy for functionality. Furthermore, the AI we envisage in this experiment reads not only the participants' but also the participants' contacts' email answers and attachments – so there is again the data externality dimension (which in one variant

85 For example, Goldfarb & Tucker 2012 use survey data with 3 million responses from 2001 to 2008 to document that older consumers are more privacy sensitive than younger consumers and that overall privacy concerns are rising over time; see A. Goldfarb & C Tucker, "Shifts in Privacy Concerns", *American Economic Review*, 2012, 102(3), 349-353.

86 Joint work with G. Mühlheußer, J. Gutmann & L. Brandimarte.

87 Goldfarb & Que, *Annual Review of Economics*, 2023, 267, pp. 272ff.

88 See, e.g., D. Cappelletti et al., "Are Default Contributions Sticky? An Experimental Analysis of defaults in Public Goods Provision", *Journal of Economic Behavior & Organization*, 2014, 108, 331-342.

we make salient), and we are curious whether raising awareness that others' data will also be shared to enable the use of this smart product will have a restraining effect. To cater for the comparative dimension, we will compare the answers of a European and a US American subject pool.

The heterogeneity in user reactions is not least driven by the context:[89] the same piece of leaked information might result in harm in one situation but not in another. Depending on goals and purposes, we might actually be more or less willing to share our data, and, effectively, the current design of the GDPR already caters for it.[90] But does it do it right? In order to find out more about the reasons for which people are willing to share their data (possibly even for free), we are designing yet another experiment with colleagues from the Erasmus School of Economics that will inform us about this set of preferences. In collaboration with a Dutch start-up, we seek to extract differences in the willingness to share (and the underlying motives for it) for a true commercial and a social purpose in an online experiment.[91] Apart from the individual preferences, this will tell us something about how multi-purpose companies are perceived.

There are manifold routes for future research: it would be interesting to link the purpose and the externality dimension: for which purposes would I actually not mind that my data is shared by others? For those the legal regime could be more lenient. It would also be interesting to understand if the others always want to know what is happening to their data or if under certain circumstances not even that is crucial for them – so in terms of policy advice we could lift information duties. We may want to strive to differentiate data users more. It is no secret that the GDPR is not able to deal with a number of vulnerable groups: children, elderly, mentally handicapped.[92] However, as particularly vulnerable groups, these individuals are also acting and transacting online. This leads to an odd situation in which vulnerable users may often pay with their data by which they finance services that more sophisticated users who largely avoid data sharing then profit from: I am a free-rider, too, here.

---

89 Fairfield & Engel, *Duke Law Journal*, 2015, 385, 399; H. Nissenbaum, "A Contextual Approach to Privacy Online", *Daedalus*, 2011, 140(4), 32, 41.

90 For more details see the next section.

91 Joint work with D. Sisak, E. Maasland, E. Tendron & E. Dijkgraaf.

92 See F. Weber, "Zeit für Inhalte *in puncto* Daten", Editorial *Verbraucher und Recht*, 2021, 5, 161-162 and *Habilitationsvortrag* on file with the author.

Let me lastly mention the EUR project AICON,[93] which uses art to disseminate knowledge about AI in the South of Rotterdam – I collaborate in this project and contributed the idea to include an excessive 'consent'-moment at the entrance of the next exhibition and shock people during the exhibition with what can actually be done with all their data they deliberately gave away by 'signing without reading'. If you attend the exhibition, you are hereby warned …

5 Fine-Tuning Current Data Law

I will now present more in depth how the current legal regime neglects the data externality.

If we display the data-sharing exercise as a continuum from always sharing to never sharing, the GDPR plays, in particular, with opt-in and opt-out options. Opt-in means that I need to take an active decision in order for my data to be shared. 'I am being asked the question to share'. Opt-out means, on the other hand, that data is automatically processed unless I object. 'I am not being asked the question to share'. Hence, the latter regime – the opt-out – comes with less protection and facilitates data processing. Therefore, it is close to the 'always', and the more complicated 'opt-in'-regime is closer to the 'never'.

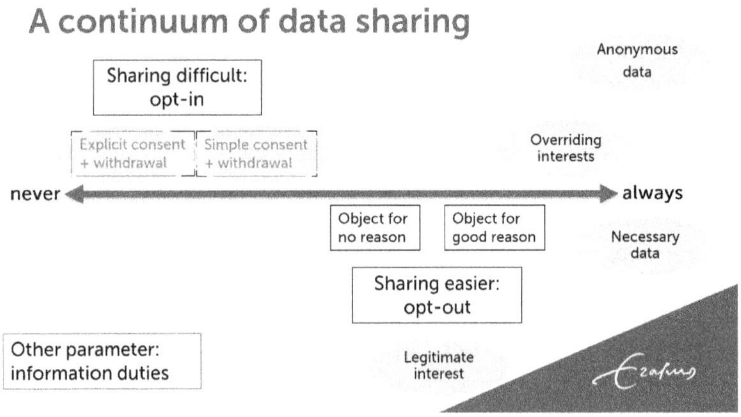

Slide 1[94]

93 See https://www.eur.nl/en/research/research-groups-initiatives/erasmus-initiatives/societal-impact-ai/aicon (last accessed 20 July 2023).

94 Slide used during inaugural lecture to exemplify.

Factoring in the type of data and context, the current data law regime can roughly[95] be subdivided into five procedures – most of which can be found in Art. 6 GDPR – and we can allocate them from right to left, so from least protected to most protected in the following way:

1. *Necessary data:*[96] This regime is governed by Art. 6(1)(b) GDPR, and if the data is necessary for the preparation or performance of a contract, it can simply be processed. To this category we can add Art. 6(1)(c) GDPR, which allows data processing if the controller needs to do this to comply with a legal obligation. Again, processing is simply possible.
2. The GDPR stipulates a number of *overriding public interests* that again allow for data processing without involving the individual in the decision (for 'normal' personal data and the elevated category of special personal data like genetic data or political opinion).[97] Objections are possible based on the very limited grounds of Art. 21(6) GDPR.
3. *Legitimate interest:*[98] To process data because of a legitimate interest, an opt-out procedure is in place – particularly known for the purpose of marketing. To be clear, companies may automatically process your personal data if they have a legitimate interest in it and inform you about the data processing and opt-out possibilities. This ground for processing boils down to a balancing exercise of company interests versus interests of the sharing individual.[99] One

95 For some aspects, Member States are also left with discretion; see, e.g., Arts. 6(2), 9(4) or 89 (2) GDPR.

96 Note that for the determination of necessity, normative considerations come into play; see B. Freund in: Schuster & Grützmacher, IT-Recht, Köln: Verlag Dr. Otto Schmidt, 2020, b) Vertrag mit der betroffenen Person – Art. 6 (1)(1)(b), para. 27.

97 See Art. 6(1)(d) GDPR for the protection of vital interests of data subject or other person, such as physical integrity, see J. Taeger in: Taeger & Gabel, DSGVO - BDSG - TTDSG, Frankfurt am Main: Deutscher Fachverlag GmbH, Fachmedien Recht und Wirtschaft, 2022, Art. 6 Rechtmäßigkeit der Verarbeitung, paras 91: this ground is to play a subsidiary role only if other grounds for data processing are not applicable. There are more examples of overriding interests linked to the category of special personal data; see Art. 9(2) (b) and following GDPR: e.g., if necessary in the context of employment and social security and social protection law (b), vital interests where the data subject is physically or legally incapable of giving consent (c), legitimate activities of foundations, associations or other not-for-profit bodies – inside these bodies only (d), data already manifestly made public (e), certain court activities (f), necessary for reasons of substantial public interest (g), preventive or occupational medicine (h) + (3), public interests in the area of public health (i), other public interest, scientific or historical research purposes or statistical purposes (j).

98 To which public authorities are excluded.

99 See Jacquemain/Klein/Mühlenbeck/Pabst/Pieper/Schwartmann in: Schwartmann Jaspers/Thüsing/Kugelmann, DS-GVO/BDSG, Heidelberg: C.F. Müller, 2020, Art. 6 Rechtmäßigkeit der Verarbeitung, paras. 152; B. Freund in: Schuster & Grützmacher, IT-Recht, Köln: Verlag Dr. Otto Schmidt, 2020, b) Vertrag mit der betroffenen Person – Art. 6(1)(1)(f), para. 39 and para. 47.

important criterion in this weighing is the question of whether it was foreseeable to the individual from the affected group that this data would be processed.[100] So the initial decision is made by the company, but the user can opt out.[101] There are some nuances as to the opt-out procedure – so how to stop this. In relation to marketing purposes, the data subject has the right to object at any time without giving any reason (see Art. 21(2) GDPR) – for other legitimate interests a 'good reason' is needed. While this provision gained a bad reputation for coming across as a loophole for marketing purposes,[102] it can actually reduce the burden for other purposes (such as in the context of research) too. It is noteworthy that it also reduces the burden for the data user if an opt-out regime is preferred over an opt-in regime. Note that Art. 6(1)(e) GDPR – a task carried out in the public interest or in exercise of public authority – follows the same opt-out regime as legitimate expectations other than marketing as stipulated in Art. 21(1) GDPR.

4. *Consent*: Below the standards of 1 and 2 and unless the legitimate interest reasoning is applicable, all other data may only be processed once an individual has consented to sharing it for a predetermined specific purpose.[103] This is, in essence, an opt-in procedure. It is noteworthy that withdrawal is possible at any time, hence, to opt-out again later (see Art. 7(3) 1st sentence GDPR). For both – consent and withdrawal – detailed procedural rules are specified. Both procedures must be equally easy.
5. *Lastly, explicit consent*: For the special categories of personal data the opt-in procedure needs to comply with elevated formalities (e.g. a signature).[104] Obviously, withdrawal is likewise possible. Even for the simple variant of consent it holds that pre-ticking is not allowed,[105] but active ticking also does not always seem to be enough. In that sense there is a grey line between consent and explicit consent.

I would like to add as a category '0' the regime for *anonymous data*, which is outside the scope of the GDPR and, hence, not granted any protection.

100 J. Taeger in: Taeger & Gabel, DSGVO – BDSG – TTDSG, Frankfurt am Main: Deutscher Fachverlag GmbH, Fachmedien Recht und Wirtschaft, 2022, Art. 6 Rechtmäßigkeit der Verarbeitung, para. 143.
101 See Art. 21(1) and (2) GDPR.
102 And also the use of deceptive designs; see L. Kye et al., "Investigating Deceptive Design in GDPR's Legitimate Interest", *CHI '23*, April 23-28, 2023, Hamburg, Germany.
103 Art. 6(1)(a) and 7 GDPR.
104 See Art. 9(2)(a) GDPR.
105 See CJEU, Case C-673/17 of 1 October 2019, ECLI:EU:C:2019:801 – *Planet49 GmbH*.

Information duties apply to any processing of personal data (hence, except for anonymous data) as stipulated in Article 13 GDPR (for the direct controller) and 14 GDPR (for third parties controlling).[106] An adherence to the general principles of the GDPR is also always of the essence.

This picture shows how the consent and legitimate interest route can often be found on websites [here, as usual, wrongly presented as alternatives[107]]:

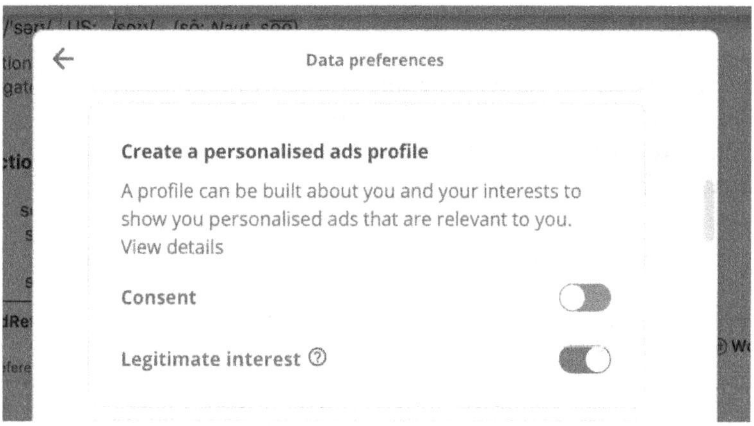

You can decide to consent. The company decided that it has a legitimate interest in processing your personal data and pre-ticked this box.

This regime is clearly tailored to an individual and his or her own data. It neglects the dimension of direct sharing of others' data and shows strong weaknesses when it comes to the dimension of indirect sharing of others' data. This is also true if we look at profiling:[108] profiling, in short, means to use personal data to predict certain characteristics or behaviour of an individual. It is, hence, tailored to the sharing

106 An exemption from information duties is only possible in highly exceptional circumstances, according to Art. 14(6) GDPR.

107 But see also the additional arguments in J. Taeger in: Taeger & Gabel, DSGVO - BDSG - TTDSG, Frankfurt am Main: Deutscher Fachverlag GmbH, Fachmedien Recht und Wirtschaft, 2022, Art. 6 Rechtmäßigkeit der Verarbeitung, para. 47.

108 According to the GDPR definition, 'profiling' means any form of automated processing of personal data consisting of the use of personal data to evaluate certain personal aspects relating to a natural person, in particular to analyse or predict aspects concerning that natural person's performance at work, economic situation, health, personal preferences, interests, reliability, behaviour, location or movements. The GDPR distinguishes between profiling used to make automated decisions and profiling as a stand-alone activity.

individual, and consent or legitimate interest are viable options for such processing (with the respective withdrawal options).[109] In neglecting the externality dimension various undesirable behavioural incentives are set that lead to bad market outcomes. Arguably, both the companies (in GDPR terminology: the controller[110]) and the sharing user can currently profit from the lack of consideration of the others' dimension.[111] The companies have an incentive to widely collect data beyond the consenting individual's data.[112] Where people pay for a service with their data, part of the price paid is actually other people's data.[113] In economic terms users overuse services.[114] In short, companies collect too much, and sharing individuals share too much.

As our main experimental outcome this far, we can – for a specific scenario – state that awareness of externalities does affect individual behaviour – we do care – and this calls for more options of enabling individuals to show this behaviour!

In the following I will make some recommendations by reinterpreting, or actually correctly interpreting, the current data rules. After a few general observations I will consider indirect and direct sharing of others' data more specifically.

When looking at the definition of 'affected' as the precondition of consent I would argue that one can actually quite convincingly also subsume 'the other' under the scope of the GDPR. So the current neglect is no necessity. The Dutch text variant uses '*betrokken*' and the German '*betroffen*' to signal the requirement of consent for personal data sharing of any affected person really, hence, also the other![115] And on that basis we may be able to close the current legal gap.

---

109 Clearly personalised price discrimination does not fall under legitimate interest.

110 Art. 4(7) GDPR.

111 De Brouwer, *Internet Policy Review*, 2020, 1, 4.

112 Ibid., 1, pp. 9, 10: economic incentives to exploit and monetise them are a given.

113 De Brouwer, *Internet Policy Review*, 2020, 1, 7.

114 Ibid., 1, 9. This would imply that users at least understand how much of their own data they give. This is likely to be underappreciated, too, compared with a situation where one would pay with money and, hence, the perception of the costs is affected twice: no understanding of how valuable the own data is that one is sharing and no understanding that on top the provider gathers also others' data.

115 See Art. 4(11) GDPR for the consent option. A similar reasoning seems appropriate when it comes to the legitimate interest provision. Also, the other grounds need to be read in light of the data subjects whose personal data are being processed.

The GDPR does vary the conditions under which certain data points can be shared. However, some fine-tuning may be in order. Scholars have claimed that markets that generate massive negative externalities need to be shut down.[116] We can see that the 'share never' category on the continuum is not used. Opening up this category is worth a consideration in the light of negative externalities. A candidate may be in the category of special data.

The existence of both negative and positive externalities, which in part only become clear over time, calls for some flexibility in the interpretation of the GDPR routes.[117] This may be a given wherever vague terms like 'legitimate interest' and 'public interest' are used. Arguably, even more flexibility to correctly intervene in specific market situations may be needed to cater accurately for the societal needs, also if we think of new developments in AI technology.

5.1 My Data and Indirect Sharing of Others' Data

My data sharing and indirect sharing of others' data is inevitably linked.[118] The main way to reduce indirect data sharing, therefore, seems to be to reduce over-sharing by individuals of their own data. A viable consent-regime remains a challenge for this (also because

116 Acemoglu et al., *Economic Journal: Microeconomics*, 2022, 218, pp. 240ff; a ban in Choi et al., *Journal of Public Economics*, 2019, 113, 121.

117 Along those lines, MacCarthy, *Journal of Law and Policy for the Information Society*, 2011, 425 with his suggestions for fine-tuning the US American system. He seeks to complement the consent option with an unfairness provision based on the degree of social utility requiring policymakers to review the outcome of information sharing in the light of data externalities. MacCarthy refers to other scholars' work that proposed other – partly related – solutions prior to him; see pp. 492ff; p. 484: "The interpretation of this statutory mandate involves the use of a three part test: (1) Does the act or practice cause substantial injury to consumers? (2) Can this injury be reasonably avoidable by consumers? (3) Are there countervailing benefits to consumers or to competition? This three part test is essentially a reduction of the concept of unfairness to a cost-benefit test. Information provision also plays a role in her system."; Ben Shahar, *Journal of Legal Analysis*, 2019, 104, 134: The challenge with command-and-control type of intervention is that it has to be determined in advance which data use is net socially harmful to forbid or not; due to the lack of a working system being developed in the US, Hirsch, *Maryland Law Review*, 2020, 439-505 reinstates the need to fine-tune the unfairness approach with the American variant of the consent issue, suggesting a move to a social protection model in light of predictive analytics; see Hirsch, *Maryland Law Review*, 2020, 439-505.

118 MacCarthy, *Journal of Law and Policy for the Information Society*, 2011, 425, 493: "As we have seen above, the presence of negative privacy externalities can mean that some information practices are harmful, even when they meet the criterion of informed consent." The informed consent option is irrelevant to the data pollution problem, says Ben Shahar, *Journal of Legal Analysis*, 2019, 104, 148.

we may never really grasp what could happen to our data[119]) – but some websites do manage at least a simple and promising yes/no question about excessive data sharing.[120] The GDPR forbids data to be processed beyond the purpose for which it was shared.[121] But reality shows the use of wide rather than specific purposes, seemingly to allow also future ideas for processing companies to come up. A clear example of unlawful processing of others' data is the Cambridge Analytica scandal:[122] to inform political advertising campaigns, the company not only harvested personal data of hundreds of thousands of users who were paid to take a personality test, but also collected data of these users' unaware Facebook friends. So to reduce data pollution by over-sharing data we need to make the purpose limitation when consenting meaningful, by making it narrower and more specific: the purpose needs to be more clearly limited to the individual at hand. Having raised your awareness of the societal costs of data sharing, I invite you to reconsider – next time you see a cookie banner – how quickly you accept excessive data sharing. By accepting the necessary cookies only, we can all contribute to reducing data externalities and its negative societal consequences. Think how much you like and trust the website that you are on... having said that, you might still be willing to signal to the world that you follow me on SSRN, researchgate, LinkedIn, etc.

As regards the opt-out regime of legitimate interests, it is noteworthy that there are more or less awareness-raising regimes. Some websites immediately list the data they process based on legitimate interests, pre-tick them and provide a direct opt-out-option. With other websites this is more hidden. In terms of information duties the GDPR stipulates that the legitimate interests need to be communicated (see Art. 13(1)(d)). Furthermore, Article 21(4) regulates that 'at the latest at the time of the first communication with the data subject' the opt-out

119 Regarding the lack of understanding, MacCarthy, *Journal of Law and Policy for the Information Society*, 2011, 425, 428; Calo, *Indiana Law Journal*, 2011, 1, 19. Many insights from behavioural law and economics can be consulted to support this point.

120 Among which the 'ec.europa.eu'-websites of the European Union.

121 J. Taeger in: Taeger & Gabel, DSGVO - BDSG - TTDSG, Frankfurt am Main: Deutscher Fachverlag GmbH, Fachmedien Recht und Wirtschaft, 2022, Art. 6 Rechtmäßigkeit der Verarbeitung, paras 45: see only very few exceptions for science, for instance, from this principle.

122 See www.theguardian.com/news/2018/mar/17/cambridge-analytica-facebook-influence-us-election (last accessed 5 July 2023); see relatedly how Ben Shahar, *Journal of Legal Analysis*, 2019, 104, 113 is concerned about the integrity of the voting process as an infected public interest. Note that in this example Cambridge Analytica is effectively a third party to the relation between Facebook and its users, a scenario that is beyond the scope of this contribution.

regime needs to be 'explicitly brought to the attention of the data subject and shall be presented clearly and separately from any other information'. In which situations can the legitimate interest-ground be used? Marketing is specifically mentioned, but, in principle, it stretches to any data use we can expect and where the balancing of interests has been adhered to. As regards the opt-out regime for legitimate interests, the balancing exercise weighing the company and the data user interests is currently only about the sharing individual. But since this is not where companies seem to stop, I would argue that it is desirable to include the externality dimension in this exercise.[123] This is my second recommendation. So it should matter whether the company has a legitimate interest in making inferences about others, too. We need to look beyond the group of the directly sharing individuals. Including this would presumably limit cases in which the company interest eventually outweighs those of sharing individuals and data losers. Whenever the company's interests would ultimately prevail in light of weighing them against those of the sharing individuals and data losers, we may still need to discuss the information duties towards the data losers.

Extensive data processing is possible with a view to anonymous data, and on top of this it is often questioned how anonymous this data really is.[124] So, thirdly, to effectively reduce excessive data processing I would suggest that it is restricted more.

Having said that, for all three cases we need to filter out scenarios of positive externalities to decide if we want to treat them differently.

123 Currently on the interest of third-party processors are considered in the exercise, see J. Taeger in: Taeger& Gabel, DSGVO - BDSG - TTDSG, Frankfurt am Main: Deutscher Fachverlag GmbH, Fachmedien Recht und Wirtschaft, 2022, Art. 6 Rechtmäßigkeit der Verarbeitung, para 126. The balancing exercise looks at the objective interests of the group of affected persons in question (see paras 140), which, to my reading, is the group of the immediately affected and does not look at the category of users affected because of the externality.

124 S. Wachter, "Normative Challenges of Identification in the Internet of Things: Privacy, Profiling, Discrimination, and the GDPR", *Computer Law & Security Review*, 2018, 34, 436, 443; R. Mühlhoff, "Predictive Privacy: Collective Data Protection in the Context of Artificial Intelligence and Big Data", *Big Data & Society*, 2023, 1-14 rightly argues that a lot of the predictive use of data points also happens with anonymous samples, which is outside the GDPR.

5.2 Direct Sharing of Others' Data

The category of direct sharing of others' data is closer to our experimental outcome, where the awareness about the sharing itself and also about the harm imposed on the other through sharing was made very explicit. So let me repeat that individuals do care, and we, therefore, have to rethink (lack of) consent. There is a discussion in the literature if by way of group coordination,[125] distributed consent,[126] group consent[127] or joint controllership,[128] consent of the other that currently falls in the legal gap can become a reality. In future research I would like to contribute more to deciding in which situations the other wants to be asked a question – which is also a burden every time. This might more likely be the case when it comes to the special categories of personal data. With a view to necessary data and overriding interests choice may be less of the essence. And even abstaining from information duties may be in line with the data losers' preferences. The outcome of our purpose-research may give a first indication about the data people would even deliberately freely share. One will need to differentiate the situation of the sharing individual and the data losers, though. It seems questionable – with a view to data minimisation and true necessity – whether in truly many cases also the others' data really would likewise be as essential or covered by the overriding interest needs as the data of the sharing individual. It may rather be nice to have for the company.

In fine-tuning the GDPR, the legitimate interest provision can again play an important role: to start with, the balancing exercise needs to be extended from company and sharing individual(s) to the data loser, too. It would also be relevant if the other could have foreseen this data sharing. Note that it is – also for you after this presentation – not completely unexpected that in truly many situations individuals also share

125 Fairfield & Engel, *Duke Law Journal*, 2015, 385, pp. 389ff: leverage inequity aversion, reciprocity and normativity to lessen exploitation, positive framing to promote altruism and communication and (private) sanctions are key to group coordination – without need for government intervention.

126 J. Lovato et al., "Limits of Individual Consent and Models of Distributed Consent in Online Social Networks", *FAccT '22*, 21-24 June 2022, Seoul, Republic of Korea, 2022, pp. 2251ff.

127 A. Puri, "A Theory of Group Privacy", *Cornell Journal of Law and Public Policy*, 2021, 30(3), 477-538; L. Taylor et al., *Group Privacy: New Challenges of Data Technologies*, 2017, Dordrecht: Springer.

128 De Brouwer, *Internet Policy Review*, 2020, 1, pp. 15ff; J. Chen et al., "Who is Responsible for Data Processing in Smart Homes? Reconsidering Joint Controllership and the Household Exemption", *International Data Privacy Law*, 2020, 10(4): on how the household exemption is becoming narrower while the notion of joint controllership is widening.

data about others, about you. There is a certain element of reciprocity present with direct sharing of others' data that deserves our experimental attention in the sense that I may accept some sharing of my data by others more easily if they also tolerate my doing the same. However, in which contexts would this be the case?

Just a few days after its fifth birthday I made a number of recommendations to improve incentives set by the GDPR to correct bad market outcomes.

6 Conclusion

What to share? About myself and about others and in which situations? It is an ongoing question.

Since this is not a retirement speech, I have included research that I have done and future ideas about experimental insights we need to write future-proof data law. It is clear that there are many eminent challenges.

Data and data law is an exciting topic of its own, but it is also clearly interlinked with other legal fields, among which are my other two favourites: consumer and competition law. I just want to give one argument each why the data externality dimension is crucial for both consumer and competition law as well:

- It is relevant for competition law that processing data beyond the consenting individual strengthens the company's market position, possibly aggravating competition law concerns on digital markets.
- For consumer law it seems relevant that excessive data sharing enhances possibilities of price discrimination.

'To share or not to share' is obviously inspired by Shakespeare's words 'to be or not to be'.[129] Does sharing these days actually mean being? It seems to be difficult in the digital and interconnected world to avoid data sharing. Sharing ensures my being. Social media gives me, furthermore, lots of opportunity to share what or who I would like to be. I can negatively affect someone else's being with what I share about them. *Hamlet* wonders in the end about 'life and death' and, by the way, also complains about 'the law's delay'. To share or not to share – an existential question just like Hamlet's?

129 Hamlet: 'To Be Or Not To Be, That Is The Question', Act III, scene 1.

I wish to thank the Board of the University for the trust they place in me with this appointment. I would like to thank the current Dean, Professor Harriët Schelhaas, and the Board of Erasmus School of Law for their support. I also wish to thank the previous Dean, Professor Suzan Stoter, for making my appointment possible. It was in the first job interview out of two that she told me – no matter the outcome – I would always have a home at Erasmus School of Law. And, indeed, coming back to Rotterdam, after having ventured out to Hamburg University (and some other short stops) for 7 years, felt exactly like coming back home. Despite corona times...

I want to take a moment to thank my scientific parents: my fabulous *Doktorvater* Professor Michael Faure, who continuously supported me throughout all these years, and my fantastic *Doktorvater* Professor Willem van Boom. Roger (van den Bergh), I am very proud to now count as your successor (even if today I talked very little about competition or consumer law... but many pages written elsewhere can be consulted). I want to thank the Rotterdam Institute of Law and Economics for welcoming me back with open arms. I also enjoy the interaction within our new big department 'Law and Business' and colleagues in other departments.

Very many thanks go, furthermore, to my female role model, my *Habilmutter* Professor Astrid Stadler, for her scientific guidance but also her advice in navigating the German market and proudly going back to the Netherlands.

I would like to thank my family and friends.

Dear friends, thank you for coming and keeping the friendships despite the distance.

Webervögel, ihr seid großartig!

Adrià, han estat 7 anys increïbles amb tu i ara estic disposada a compartir-te amb una altra personeta.

Ik heb gezegd – of eigenlijk: wij.

www.ingramcontent.com/pod-product-compliance
Lightning Source LLC
Chambersburg PA
CBHW061357240926
51846CB00007B/1434